Vegan Casseroles Cookbook

All about veggie food and Vegan casseroles recipes

Bobby Flatt

INTRODUCTION

Vegan cuisine has become an uprising trend in present world. This is a kind of cuisine in which no meat or any meat tissue is used. If you have to make it pure vegan, you will not even use egg and milk in your dish. The people who are not able to follow pure vegan, use dairy product and egg and are known as lacto-ovo-vegan. There are a few categories of food that comes under vegan food category like tofu, soy products, vegetables, fruits, herbs and other non- animal related products.

The book, vegan casserole recipe book contains 25 recipes that are made especially for people who like vegan food. There are so many recipes in the book that contains a variety of ingredients, right from vegetables to tofu. We have tried to substitute meat for you with mushroom meat, tofu and many other ingredients. The dishes are designed by keeping in mind the taste and health of all the people who like vegan food. There are a few contents in meat like protein which is available in abundance to meat eaters. These contents are missing in diet of vegan eaters. To compensate the vegans, we have used appropriate ingredients so that vegan eaters do not remain deficient in any kind of nutrient.

The recipes are simple, easy and fun to make. A lot of innovation is done in all these recipes so that you get something that is tasty and unusual. You will definitely love making all the recipes because they are made in few easy steps. Do you now want to jump into these delicious recipes and try out all at once? Have a happy cooking!

TABLE OF CONTENTS

INTRODUCTION 2

VEGAN SOUP, SALAD AND DIP 6

GINGER AND CARROT SOUP 7

CURRY SOUP 9

ASPARAGUS SOUP 11

THAI SALAD AND PEANUT 13

RAINBOW SALAD 16

TORTILLA SOUP 19

CHIPOTLE DIP 21

VEGAN APPETIZER 23

PENNE PASTA 24

CHILI WITH EXTRA VEGGIES 26

MUSHROOM MEAT WITH NACHOS 28

QUESADILLAS OF SWEET POTATO AND KALE 30

BAKED ZITI 32

YUMMY MANGO FAJITAS 34

MAIN COURSE 36

SHIPWRECK CASSEROLE IN VEGETARIAN STYLE 37

BLACK BEAN AND MUSHROOM TORTILLA 39

QUINOA BROCCOLI CASSEROLE 41

RICOTTA PASTA WITH PUMPKIN 44

VEGETABLE CASSEROLE IN GREEK STYLE 47

BROWN RICE, SPINACH AND CHEESE CASSEROLE 49

DESSERT 51

RASPBERRY AND CREAMY SMOOTHIE 52

GREEN ORANGE SMOOTHIE 54

NANAIMO BAR 56

VEGAN PECAN PIE 59

MINI VEGAN PIE 61

CRANBERRY CAKE 63

VEGAN SOUP, SALAD AND DIP

GINGER AND CARROT SOUP

The soup is simply delicious and has a lot of flavors of vegetables. It is super simple to make and can become your best buddy at times of cool winters. The dish simply awesome!

Preparation Time: 45 minutes
Serving Size: 4

INGREDIENTS:

- Carrots, peeled and cut in long strips- 7
- Potatoes, peeled and cut in chunks- 2
- Onion, chopped- 1
- Garlic cloves, chopped- 2
- Fresh ginger, grated- 1 inch piece
- Coconut oil- 3 tsp
- Vegetable stock- 1 1/2 cups
- Water- 2 1/2 cups
- Salt- 1 tsp
- Maple syrup- 2 tbsp.
- Lemon juice- 1/2 tbsp.

DIRECTIONS:

1. Prepare oven to 425 degrees F
2. Take a pan and add 2 tsp of coconut oil in the pan. Add all the carrot in the pan. Once carrot is tossed for a minute transfer it to the baking dish.
3. Roast the carrots in oven for about 20 minutes and you will find them very crispy.
4. Take a saucepan and add rest of coconut oil in the pan. Heat the oil and then add ginger, garlic and onion in the oil. Sauté the ingredients for about 3 minutes or till onion get translucent.
5. Add vegetable stock and water in the saucepan. Let it simmer for a minute. Now add carrot, potato and salt in the saucepan. Cook all the ingredients till you find potato going tender.
6. Put off the flame and add all the ingredients to a blender. Add some lemon juice, maple syrup and blend everything in the blender. Make a smooth paste out of it. Your soup is ready to be served. If you like your soup less thick then you can add more water in it.

CURRY SOUP

The name of the soup is a name enough to tell you about the kind of taste this soup will bear. It has lot of vegetables in it. It has tofu to provide consistency to the soup.

Preparation Time: 25 minutes
Serving Size: 6

INGREDIENTS:

- Vegetable broth- 6cups
- Ginger, peeled and sliced- 1 inch
- White mushrooms, sliced- 8 oz.
- Hard tofu, cut into cubes- 14 oz.
- Light coconut milk- 13.5 oz.
- Red curry paste- 3 tbsp.
- Brown sugar- 2-3 tsp
- Green onions- sliced
- Cilantro
- Basil leaves- 6
- Lime wedges- 6

DIRECTIONS:

1. Take a bowl and put broth and ginger in it. Let the two come to boil on high heat.
2. Once broth starts boiling, take the ginger piece out and add tofu and mushroom. Cook the two ingredients over medium flame. Cook the two for about 5 minutes and see if the mushroom has softened or not.
3. Now add coconut milk, brown sugar and curry paste in the bowl. Take the soup out and serve it with cilantro, basil, green onion and lime wedges as garnishing on the top.

ASPARAGUS SOUP

This soup will not take long to be cooked neither you will need a lot of toppings to make this one perfect. This is a simple recipe with full of fresh flavor of Asparagus. A pinch of cashews will add some protein content in this soup. If you love asparagus then this becomes a definite try.

Preparation Time: 30 minutes
Serving Size: 6

INGREDIENTS:

- Cashew pieces- 2/3 cup
- Olive oil- 1 tbsp.
- Large onion, sliced- 1
- Garlic, minced- 2 cloves
- Sweet curry powder- 1tbsp
- Asparagus, cut into 1.5 inch pieces- 32Oz
- Vegetable broth- 6 cups
- Salt- 1/2tbsp
- Pepper to taste
- Lemon wedges for serving

DIRECTIONS:

1. Take a bowl and fill it with hot water. Put cashew pieces in this bowl. Cover the bowl and keep it aside.
2. Take a Dutch oven and heat oil in that oven over medium heat. Add onion in it and cook onion for about 5 minutes. Add curry powder and garlic to the ingredient for 2 minutes.
3. Add broth and asparagus to this oven and let it boil for some time over low heat. Cook all the ingredients for about 15 minutes and within this time asparagus will soften a bit. Put off the flame and let soup cool down for some time.
4. Take a blender and add some cashew pieces and the cooled down soup in a blender bowl. Blend all the contents properly in the blender. Put all the content in the Dutch oven and warm the soup a bit. Sprinkle some pepper and salt on the top. Squeeze some lime juice on the top. Serve the soup hot.

THAI SALAD AND PEANUT

There are just two steps in making of this salad but then preparation that goes behind making it perfect is some skill. One tip I will give you is that have a good cutting knife. It will make your preparation very easy.

Preparation Time: 25 minutes
Serving Size: 4

INGREDIENTS:

For the salad:
- Tomato, quartered - 1
- Yellow bell pepper, thinly sliced- 1
- Red bell pepper, thinly sliced- 1
- Green bell pepper, thinly sliced- 1
- Serrano pepper, thinly sliced- 1
- Carrots, peeled and sliced- ¼ cup
- Papaya, finely chopped- 1
- Bamboo shoots, finely chopped- ¼ cup
- Peanuts, roughly roasted- ¼ cup
- Scallions, thinly sliced- 3

For the dressing:
- Sesame oil- 1 tsp
- Peanut butter- 2 tbsp.
- Brown sugar- 2 tbsp.
- Garlic, chopped- 2 cloves
- Ginger, diced- 1 tbsp
- Lemongrass- ½ tsp
- Red chili pepper, crushed- 1
- Soy sauce- 2 tsp
- Lime juice- 1 tbsp.
- Cilantro for garnishing

DIRECTIONS:

1. Take a bowl and mix all the ingredients that are present in salad column.
2. Take a saucepan and put it on medium flame. Put sesame oil in the pan and warm it for a minute. In this pan add ginger and garlic. Let the two cook for a minute till they soften.

3. In this pan add all the ingredients that belong to dressing section. Cook all the ingredients nicely.
4. Take the salad bowl and add the dressing thus prepared on the top of salad. Mix everything properly.
5. Have freshly made salad

RAINBOW SALAD

The name is enough to give a hint on the kind of ingredients that are present in this salad. There are a lot of veggies, there is quinoa and there is creamy avocado in this dish. Have a great weekend preparing this one with family and have a sumptuous breakfast.

Preparation Time:　　50 minutes
Serving Size:　　4

INGREDIENTS:

For the veggies:
- Red onion, finely sliced- 1
- Red pepper, finely sliced- 1
- Green pepper, finely sliced- 1
- Zucchini, diced – 1 small
- Butternut squash cubed into ¾ inch size- 4 cups
- Olive oil- 2 tbsp.
- Salt- ¾ tsp
- Pepper- ¼ tsp

For the dressing:
- Avocado, sliced- 1
- Greek yogurt- 2 tbsp.
- Apple cider vinegar- 1 tsp
- Olive oil- 2 tbsp.
- Milk- ½ cup
- Salt- ¼ tsp
- Chives, minced - 1 ½ tbsp.
- Fresh dill- 1 tsp

For the salad:
- Mixed greens- 5 oz
- Cooked quinoa, cold- 2 ¾ to 3 cups
- Sunflower seeds- ¼ cup
- Walnuts, finely chopped- ½ cup

DIRECTIONS:

To make the veggies:
1. Prepare the oven at 375ºF
2. Take a baking dish and put both kinds of pepper, onion, zucchini and butternut squash in the dish. Spray olive oil on

the top and put some salt and pepper from the top. Mix all the ingredients properly and make an even layer in the dish.
3. Put this dish in oven and cook ingredients for about 30 minutes. After first 15 minutes, stir contents once and let it cook for another 15 minutes. Take the dish out and keep it aside for 10 minutes.

To make the dressing:

1. Take a bowl and add Greek yogurt, avocado, olive oil, vinegar, milk and salt in the bowl. Combine everything properly. Put the ingredients in a blender and blend it properly. Once done, add chives and dill in the blender. If you like the dressing to be less consistent then add more milk in it.
2. Take a bowl and add some mixed green in the bowl. On top of it add some quinoa in the bowl. Then add roasted veggies and sprinkle some walnuts and sunflower seeds. At last add the required amount of dressing on the top. Mix well and your salad is ready.

TORTILLA SOUP

The soup is delicious in itself. However, the best part about this soup is that it can be served with a multiple toppings which add to overall taste of the soup. You can add toppings like sour cream, pickled jalapenos, fresh tomato, red onion and a few more. The best one is tortilla, behind which the soup has been named.

Preparation Time: 40 minutes
Serving Size: 6

INGREDIENTS:

- Canola oil- 3 tbsp.
- Yellow onion, finely chopped- 1
- Green pepper, finely chopped- 1/2
- Yellow pepper, finely chopped- 1/2
- Jalapeno, seeded and sliced-1
- Garlic cloves, diced- 3
- Tomato paste- 2tbsp
- Cumin- 1 1/2tbsp
- Oregano- 1 tsp
- Ancho chile- 1 1/2tbsp
- Tomatoes- 1 20oz
- Vegetable broth- 6 cups
- Zucchini, chopped- 1
- Hominy, cooked- 1 cup
- Black beans, cooked - 1 cup
- Cilantro, chopped- 2tbsp
- Lime juice- 1/2

DIRECTIONS:

1. Take a large soup pot and put some oil in the pot. Let the oil warm in the pot for about 1 minute.
2. In this pot add some bell pepper, jalapeno and onion and let it cook for about 5 minutes. Cook them till vegetable softens.
3. Now add tomato paste, cumin, garlic, oregano and ancho. Let it sauté for about 3 minutes. Now add tomato with juice and let it simmer for about 10 minutes.
4. Add Zucchini, black beans and hominy in the pot and let all the ingredients simmer for about 10 more minutes.
5. Once soup has been cooked properly, remove it from heat and add some lime juice and cilantro in it. Serve with tortilla strips if you like.

CHIPOTLE DIP

This dip goes well with any kind of appetizer and can be transported to any place easily. So, next time when you have a port lunch at your office then do carry this dip along and spice up your whole special lunch.

Preparation Time: 4 hours 40 minutes
Serving Size: 16

INGREDIENTS:

- Olive oil- 1 tsp
- Yellow onion, chopped- 1
- Black beans, washed and drained- 15Oz
- Paprika, smoked - 1 tsp
- Chili powder- 1 tbsp.
- Salsa- ½ cup
- Green chili- 4Oz
- Chipotle paste- 1 tsp
- Pinto beans, washed and drained- 15 Oz
- Cheese, grated- ½ cup

DIRECTIONS:

1. Take a medium size skillet and heat oil in the skillet. Add onion and cook it for about 30 minutes so that onion is caramelized properly. You can add some water to caramelize onion properly. Cook till everything becomes brown.
2. Take a bowl and add black beans, chili powder, onion, salsa, smoked paprika, chipotle paste and green chili. Mix all the ingredients well.
3. Take pinto bean in slow cooker and mash it with masher. On this mixture place black bean and cheese. Cover this cooker and cook slowly for about 4 hours till it becomes hot.
4. Serve the dip with chips or freshly sliced veggies.

VEGAN APPETIZER

PENNE PASTA

This one is an easy and delicious recipe that can be prepared in just about 25 minutes. A perfect way to start off your day. It has broccolini in it; it has cheese in it and has dried tomatoes. This is a perfect way of getting a lot of flavors in morning time.

Preparation Time: 25
Serving Size: 4

INGREDIENTS:

- Wheat penne, cooked- 8 oz.
- Broccolini, trimmed from ends- 1 bunch
- Extra-virgin olive oil- 2 tbsp.
- Garlic cloves, finely sliced- 2
- Pine nuts- 2 tbsp.
- Red chili flakes- ½ tsp
- Sun-dried tomatoes, sliced- 1/2 cup
- Salt
- Pepper
- Parmesan cheese, shredded- 5 tbsp.

DIRECTIONS:

1. Take a bowl and cook penne as mentioned in the packet. Just when penne is about to be cooked put broccolini in the bowl. When both ingredients are cooked well, drain them out and keep aside.
2. Take iron skillet and put oil in the skillet. Let the oil warm a little. Now add garlic in the oil and let it cook for 2 minutes.
3. Now put red pepper flakes and pine nut in the skillet. Cook all the ingredients for about 2 minutes. Now add dried tomatoes and pasta in the skillet. Cook for about 1 minute. At last add broccolini in the skillet and sprinkle some salt and pepper on the top.
4. Remove the skillet from heat and garish it with parmesan cheese on the top. Serve the delicious pasta.

CHILI WITH EXTRA VEGGIES

This is a perfect appetizer for someone who loves to eat a lot of chilies at the start of the day. You can add some beans in this dish but if you have to make it really healthy and tasty then follow this recipe to the toe and have a sumptuous and tasty snack, any time of day. You can store this in freezer for later use.

Preparation Time: 55 minutes
Serving Size: 4

INGREDIENTS:

- Olive oil- 2 tbsp.
- Medium onion, sliced- 1
- Garlic, diced- 1 clove
- Chili powder- 1tbsp
- Cumin- 2 tsp
- Dried oregano- 2 tsp
- Cayenne pepper- 1/8-1/4 teaspoon
- Zucchini, minced- 1
- Yellow squash, sliced- 1 small
- Red pepper, sliced- 1
- Tomatoes with green chili flakes, diced- 20Oz
- Tomato paste- 2 tbsp.
- Corn, taken out kernels - 1 ear
- Black bean, cooked - 1 1/2 cups
- Kidney beans, cooked - 1 1/2 cups
- Salt to taste
- Pepper to taste

DIRECTIONS:

1. Take a Dutch oven and heat oil over low flame in it. Once the oil is heated add onion in it. Let it cook and get softened for about 7 minutes. Once onion is cooked add cumin, oregano, garlic, chili and cayenne in the oven. Let all the ingredients cook for about 1 minute.
2. Now add yellow squash, red pepper and zucchini in the oven and let it cook till all the ingredients are softened. This should take about 10 minutes.
3. Once these are cooked, add tomato paste, tomatoes, bean and corn in the oven. Let all the ingredients simmer in low temperature for about 20 minutes. Sprinkle some pepper and salt on the top.
4. Your appetizer is ready to be served.

MUSHROOM MEAT WITH NACHOS

When it is time to go vegan there are a lot of innovations that we do in our cooking. A lot of substitution happens, like in this one. Instead of normal meat we are making meat out of mushroom. You will definitely like doing this innovation with mushrooms.

Preparation Time: 25 minutes
Serving Size: 4

INGREDIENTS:

Portabella Mushroom Meat
- Olive oil- 1 tbsp.
- Small onion, finely chopped- 1
- Garlic, diced- 1 clove
- Cumin, grounded- 1 tsp
- Paprika, smoked - 1 tsp
- Portabella mushrooms, chopped- 3
- Chipotle pepper, minced- 1 tbsp.
- Salt and pepper

Loaded Veggie Nachos
- Tortilla chips
- Sautee Vegetables like red pepper, green pepper and Zucchini- $1/4^{th}$ cup
- Jalapeno- 1 tsp
- Green Onion- 1tbsp

DIRECTIONS:

Portabella Mushroom Meat
1. Take a large skillet and heat oil over medium flame in it. Once oil gets warm add onion in it till it softens. This should take about 3 minutes.
2. Once onion is cooked, add cumin, paprika and garlic in it. Cook for another one minute. Now add chipotle and mushroom in it till mushroom leaves liquid. This should take about 8 minutes. Take the skillet from flame and toss some salt and pepper on the top.
3. Take nachos and top the above prepared meat and also put some of other topping as mentioned. Serve the snack.

QUESADILLAS OF SWEET POTATO AND KALE

To bind every ingredient properly in Quesadillas, traditionally, cheese is used. We have changed the recipe a bit and have instead used sweet potato to do the trick to make the dish healthier for you. The combination of sweet potato and kale is a must try.

Preparation Time: 1 hour 30 minutes
Serving Size: 4

INGREDIENTS:

- Sweet potato, poked with knife - 1
- Olive oil- 1 tbsp.
- Large onion- 1
- Kale, chopped- 1 1/2 cups
- Vegetarian chorizo sausage, grated- 1
- Salt to taste
- Pepper to taste
- Black beans, cooked- ½ cup
- Paprika, smoked- ½ tsp
- Olive oil as cooking spray
- Wheat tortillas- 4
- Salsa for serving

DIRECTIONS:

1. Prepare the oven at 400 degrees
2. Take a baking sheet and line it with aluminum sheet. Place sweet potato on this foil. Cook this sweet potato for about 45 minutes. The skin will go tender and can be removed easily. Mash sweet potato nicely.
3. Take a skillet and take some oil in it. Heat the oil and add some onion in it. The onion will start caramelizing in about 50 minutes. Once this is done add chorizo to the skillet and cook for another 5 minutes. Put in kale and keep stirring till it gets wilted. Sprinkle some salt and pepper on the top.
4. Take a small bowl and mix paprika and black beans in the bowl.
5. Now take out sweet potato and divide this into two. Divide similarly caramelized onion and beans. Fill the filling into quesadillas. Cook this quesadillas in skillet on all the sides till the color changes to brown color.
6. Cut quesadillas into wedges and serve it with salsa.

BAKED ZITI

To make ziti it is not important that you add a lot of cheese in the dish. You can make it our way by adding ricotta and veggies. The dish will taste as awesome as ever. It is a must try recipe in this book.

Preparation Time: 1 hour 5 minutes
Serving Size: 6

INGREDIENTS:

- Cooking spray
- Olive oil- 1tbsp
- Onion, finely sliced- 1
- Large zucchini, finely sliced from length - 1
- Mushrooms, sliced-8 oz.
- Wheat pasta- 8 oz.
- Marinara sauce- 24 Oz
- Ricotta Cheese- 15 Oz
- Salt and pepper to taste
- Mozzarella cheese- ¼ cup
- Parsley, chopped- 1 tbsp.

DIRECTIONS:

1. Prepare oven at 350 degree F.
2. Take a baking dish of 9x13 size and spray some cooking oil in the dish.
3. Take a skillet and put some olive oil in the skillet. Heat the skillet over medium flame. Add onion in this skillet and cook for about 4 minutes till onion softens. Add mushroom and Zucchini in the skillet and cook for about 7 more minutes. Put the heat off.
4. Add pasta, ricotta, marinara sauce, pepper and salt in the skillet. Let it cook along with vegetables. Stir every content well so that everything mixes properly.
5. Pour this mixture in the baking dish and pour cheese on the top. Bake the dish for about 30 minutes. Take the dish out and serve it hot by garnishing it with parsley.

YUMMY MANGO FAJITAS

What can be more fulfilling and tastier than fajitas? Use as many toppings as you like in this wonderful dish. The best would be cilantro, fresco and lime wedges.

Preparation Time: 30 minutes
Serving Size: 4

INGREDIENTS:

- Olive oil- 1 tbsp.
- Fajita seasoning mix- 1 tbsp.
- Red onion, finely sliced- 1
- Red pepper, seed removed and sliced- 1
- Zucchini, sliced lengthwise- 1
- Jalapeño, seed removed and sliced- 1
- Mangoes, peeled and cut into chunks- 2
- Tortillas, warmed- 8
- Cilantro, salsa and lime wedges for topping

DIRECTIONS:

1. Take a skillet and heat olive oil in it over medium flame.
2. In this skillet add fajita seasoning and cook for about 30 seconds. Add onion and cook the ingredients for about 7 minutes.
3. Now add zucchini, jalapeno and red pepper can cook all the ingredients for about 5 minutes.
4. Add mango in this mixture and serve it with the toppings mentioned in the ingredients list.

MAIN COURSE

SHIPWRECK CASSEROLE IN VEGETARIAN STYLE

Vegetarian shipwreck casserole might sound something very unusual and you must be having your own doubts about the dish, however, this recipe deserves one try. It will not disappoint you. It is made perfectly keeping in mind the vegan style and taste of the dish.

Preparation Time: 1 hour 20 Minutes
Serving Size: 6-8

INGREDIENTS:

- Olive oil- 1 tbsp.
- Yellow onion, sliced- 1
- Packages tempeh, crushed- 8Oz
- Salt to taste
- Pepper to taste
- Cooking spray
- Potatoes, baked and sliced- 2
- Vegetarian Beans, Baked- 14Oz (1 can)
- Tomato Soup- 10Oz

DIRECTIONS:

1. Take your oven out and prepare it at 375 degrees.
2. Take a large skillet and put it on medium flame. Pour oil in the skillet and let it heat for some time. Once you see smoke out of oil put sliced onions in the oil and let it sauté for 8 minutes. Once you see that onion is turned golden brown and has softened add tempeh in the skillet. Cook the ingredients till you see an overall brown color. Sprinkle some salt and pepper from the top.
3. Take a baking dish of about 9 x 11 size and spray some oil on the dish. Put a layer of potatoes at the bottom of the baking dish. You can overlap the potatoes. Add some salt and pepper as seasoning.
4. On top of potato add the initially prepared tempeh mixture. On top of tempeh mixture put some baked beans. Finally put tomato soup layer at the top.
5. Do not cover the dish and put it into oven for baking for 1 hour.
6. Take the dish out and serve it hot.

BLACK BEAN AND MUSHROOM TORTILLA

This is a perfect meal for those weeknights when you need to have something light, tasty and easy to make. You will feel like you are having a lot of nachos for dinner. Mushroom, beans topped with salsa and cheese makes the dish a perfect one.

Preparation Time: 30 minutes
Serving Size: 4

INGREDIENTS:

- Extra-virgin olive oil- 2 tsp
- Button mushrooms, trimmed and sliced into chunks- 12Oz
- Garlic clove, diced- 1
- Pepper -1/4 tsp
- Salt to taste
- Pepper- ½ tsp
- Black Beans, rinsed and drained- 16 Oz
- Corn tortillas, divided into two- 8
- Salsa- 2 cups
- Tomatoes, chopped – 1 cup
- Jack Cheese, shredded- 1 ¼ cups

DIRECTIONS:

1. Prepare the oven at 400 degrees.
2. Take a skillet and add some oil in the skillet. Heat oil for a minute over high flame.
3. In the skillet add mushroom and keep stirring it for about 7 minutes till mushroom has become brown in color. Once mushroom is cooked, add cayenne and garlic. Cook all the ingredients for a minute and then add some salt and pepper. Cook ingredients for about 2 minutes and check whether beans are warm or not.
4. Take a baking dish and arrange tortilla halves, about 5 of them in the dish. On the top pour half of the bean mixture prepared earlier. On the top this bean mixture add ½ cup of salsa and the chopped tomatoes. As the top most layer, add $1/3^{rd}$ of cheese.
5. Make a similar layer of tortilla on the top of first one.
6. Take a silver foil and cover the baking dish. Bake this dish for about 10 minutes till the cheese melts. After cheese melts, uncover the dish and bake for another 5 minutes. Serve the dish hot.

QUINOA BROCCOLI CASSEROLE

A classic recipe that is comfortable for you with taste. This recipe has been turned around to be a vegan dish which tastes even better than its original version. The dish contains a lot of good fats and proteins that is very good for your health.

Preparation Time: 1 hour 15 minutes
Serving Size: 8

INGREDIENTS:

For the Vegan Cream Cheese:
- Raw cashew, soaked for 4 hours - 2 cups
- Water- ½ cup
- Lemon juice- 1tbsp
- white wine vinegar- 1tbsp
- Yeast- 1½ tbsp.
- Salt- 1tsp

For the casserole
- Broccoli cuts- 32Oz
- Crimini Mushroom, chopped- 8Oz
- Yellow onion, chopped- 1
- Sweet non-dairy milk- 3 cups
- Gluten-free flour- 3tbsp
- Quinoa, uncooked- 1cup
- Ritz Crackers, crumbled- 2 sleeves
- Olive oil- 1tbsp
- Salt and pepper to taste

DIRECTIONS:

Make the Vegan Cream Cheese
1. Take a blender and blend soaked and dried cashew.
2. In the same blender add all the other ingredients mentioned in cream section and make a smooth paste out of it.

Make the casserole
1. Prepare the oven at 359 degree F.
2. Take a large pot full of water and put it on high flame.
3. Take quinoa in a bowl and put some hot water in this bowl till a level where quinoa submerges properly.

4. Take a skillet and put it over medium heat. Once this skillet is hot add some onion and mushroom in it. Cook all ingredients for 6 minutes. Cook till onion becomes soft and you see liquid coming out of mushroom.
5. Add some flour on the skillet and make a coat over onion and mushroom.
6. Pour milk in the skillet and stir the ingredients for a minute. Let all the ingredients and milk cook on medium flame for about 5 minutes. Once milk has thickened, put off the heat.
7. Take a pot and fill it with water. Boil the water and cook broccoli in it for about 5 minutes. Once cooked, drain out all the water and store broccoli in the pot.
8. Add quinoa with broccoli in the pot. Pour mushroom soup and cheese in the pot. Stir all the ingredients for one minute. Sprinkle some salt and pepper from the top.
9. Take a casserole dish of 9x13 size and pour all the mixture in the dish.
10. Take a pan and mix sum soil and crackers in it. Now spread this mixture on top of casserole dish.
11. Put this dish in oven for about 30 minutes. Do not cover the dish. Once done you can have hot and steamy dish.

RICOTTA PASTA WITH PUMPKIN

This dish is special in its own sense. It is very creamy and light yet we have not use a lot of cheese to make it creamy. Instead pumpkin plays a very important role and substitutes extra cheese. It is healthy and tasty; what more can you ask for!!

Preparation Time: 50 minutes
Serving Size: 6

INGREDIENTS:

- Olive oil
- Pasta- 16Oz,
- Ricotta- 15Oz
- Pumpkin puree- 15Oz
- Eggs- 2
- Yogurt- 1/2 cup
- Salt- 2 tsp
- Black pepper- 1tsp
- Nutmeg, grounded- 1/2tsp
- Ginger, grounded- 1/2tsp
- Pecans, chopped- 3/4 cup
- Sage leaves, chopped- 1/2 cup
- Garlic cloves, chopped- 2
- Parmesan, grated- 3/4 cup
- Prepare oven at 375°F.

DIRECTIONS:

1. Take a pot of a size 4 quart and pour some water in the pot. Bring this water to boil over high flame. Stir in 1 tbsp. salt in the water. Cook pasta in this pot for about 10 minutes. Drain water and keep aside pasta. Toss 2tsp of olive oil in pasta.
2. Take a large bowl and mix pumpkin puree, egg, ricotta and yogurt. Whisk it properly so that every ingredient mixes well. Once ingredients get mixed, add salt, nutmeg, pepper and ginger into it.
3. Put cooked pasta in the mixture and let a coat form around pasta. In the same mixture, put pecans, sage, garlic and ½ cup cheese.
4. Prepare a baking dish by sprinkling some olive oil on the dish. Put the mixture layer evenly on the dish. Put remaining cheese

on the top. Put the dish inside oven for about 35 minutes. Do not cover the dish.
5. Once you see that the color of dish has turned golden brown, take it out. Wait for 5 minutes before serving the dish.

VEGETABLE CASSEROLE IN GREEK STYLE

There are so many veggies in this main course with so many different flavors in it. The dish has been baked to give a different flavor to the dish.

Preparation Time: 1 hour 15 minutes
Serving Size: 6

INGREDIENTS:

- Zucchini, made into 4 sections lengthwise - 8 Oz
- Red onion, cut into wedges of ½ inch size- 1 small
- Olive oil, divided- 4 tbsp.
- Kosher salt- 1 tbsp.
- Gold potatoes cut into wedges of 1 inch- 16Oz
- Green beans, trimmed- 8Oz
- Tomatoes, Peeled and quartered- 1 ¼ cups
- Garlic cloves, sliced- 4
- Lemon juice- 1tbsp
- Oregano- 1tbsp
- Fresh dill, chopped- 2 tbsp.
- Feta, crushed- 1/4 cup

DIRECTIONS:

1. Prepare oven at 450° F.
2. Take a bowl and pour 1 tbsp. of olive oil in the bowl. Put some zucchini and onion in the bowl so that they mix well with oil.
3. Take a baking dish and roast zucchini and onion for about 15 minutes in the dish. The ingredients will turn brown. Once they are brown put ingredients on wire rack.
4. Parallely, take another bowl and mix tomatoes, potato, green beans, lemon juice, garlic, oregano and 3tbsp of oil in the bowl. Sprinkle some salt from the top.
5. Take another baking dish and put the above prepared mixture in the dish. Put zucchini and onion on the top. Cover this dish with a foil and bake for about 30 minutes.
6. Take the dish out and then remove the foil. Cook all the ingredients for another 35 minutes.
7. Once cooking is done, sprinkle some dill and feta on the top. Serve the dish after 10 minutes.

BROWN RICE, SPINACH AND CHEESE CASSEROLE

This dish serves as one of the perfect vegan dishes that can be prepared without much of a planning. If you have a few ingredients, rest can be managed. If you are on a routine of no meat on Mondays, then this dish can definitely capture one of your Mondays!

INGREDIENTS:

- Brown rice- 3 cups
- Spinach, washed and chopped- 16 oz.
- Eggs- 2
- Buttermilk- 1/2 cup
- Green onions, sliced- 1/2 cup
- Dried thyme- 1 tsp
- Salt- 1/2 tsp
- Worcestershire sauce- 1/2 tsp
- Feta cheese, grated- 1 cup
- Parmesan, grated- 1/2 cup + 1/4 cup

DIRECTIONS:

1. Prepare oven at 350 degree F.
2. Take a bowl and beat eggs in the bowl. Mix some buttermilk in the bowl. Once the mixture is made, add some onion, salt, thyme and Worcestershire sauce. Mix all the ingredients well.
3. Add spinach in this mixture and top it with Feta and 3/4th Parmesan. Mix all the ingredients and at the end add brown rice to it.
4. Take a baking dish and spray oil in it. The casserole should be a size of 3 quart. Put all the ingredients in the dish and bake it for about 35 minutes.
5. Take out the dish and spread remaining parmesan on the top. Cook the dish for another 10 minutes. Your dish is ready to be served.

DESSERT

RASPBERRY AND CREAMY SMOOTHIE

If you are a raspberry fan then do try this not so tough dish at your home. The ingredients used in this smoothie will give you some extra kick of raspberry. Also, to keep it purely vegan we have used coconut milk. Enjoy delicious drink!!

Preparation Time: 15 minutes
Serving Size: 2

INGREDIENT:

- Fresh raspberries- 2 ¼ cups
- Frozen banana, peeled and cut into cubes- 1
- Raspberry preserves- 2 tbsp.
- Coconut milk yogurt- 6Oz
- Vanilla almond milk- 1 1/2 cups
- Vanilla extract- 1/4 tsp
- Ice cubes- 8
- Coconut Toasted- For garnish

DIRECTIONS:

1. Take a blender and put 2 cups of raspberries in it. Blend it properly.
2. Add rest of the ingredients except toasted coconut and $1/4^{th}$ cup raspberry. Once a fine smooth content is achieved take it out and pour it in serving glasses.
3. As a garnish add some raspberry and toasted coconut on the top. Serve it chilled.

GREEN ORANGE SMOOTHIE

This smoothie is very healthy and is tasty. You can use some orange wedges and make it more consistent, creamy and thick. It is a very easy recipe and you will love making it and tasting it.

Preparation Time: 5 minutes

Serving Size: 1 large glass

INGREDIENTS:

- Non-dairy milk with vanilla flavored- 1 cup
- Oranges, peeled, cut and frozen- 2
- Kale leaves- 5
- Sweetener as per your choice

DIRECTIONS:

1. Take a blender and combine all the ingredients in the bowl of blender. Blend all the ingredients in the bowl properly till all the chunks have been blended properly.
2. Once you receive a smooth paste, take it out and serve it in a thick glass. Your yummy dessert is ready to be served.

NANAIMO BAR

This is probably a known one in Canada, which is taken out of a name of Canadian City. This dish has been tailor made to be healthier, more vegan and much more delicious. Enjoy the triple layer bar.

Preparation Time: 50 min.
Serving Size: 12

INGREDIENTS:

Top Layer of Bar:
- Coconut oil - 2 tbsp.
- Chocolate, Dark ones - 6 oz.

Middle Layer of Bar:
- Sweetener, Granular - 4 tbsp.
- Macadamia nuts, alternatively you can use cashews - 3 cups
- Vanilla powder, alternatively you can use vegan protein - 4 tbsp.
- Coconut oil - 6 tbsp.

Bottom Layer of Bar:
- Coconut, Both shredded and unsweetened - 2 cup
- Almond meal - 1/2 cup
- Cocoa - 1/2 cup
- Coconut oil – 1/2 cup
- Granular sweetener – 1/2 cup

DIRECTIONS:

1. Base layer is the first one to go for. For this take a blender and put ingredients (Mentioned in bottom layer section), except melted coconut. Blend the contents of blender roughly so that a bit of coconut texture remains in the mixture.
2. Mix the prepared mixture with coconut oil. Use fork for mixing.
3. Then pour the prepared mixture into loaf pan and let it freeze in freezer for some time.
4. Now prepare the middle layer. Put all the ingredients present in middle layer in the blender and make a smooth paste out of all the ingredients. There should be no chunks in this layer.

5. Now pour the prepared middle layer over the first layer that we kept in freezer. Put it back again in the refrigerator.
6. Take a double boiler and melt coconut oil and chocolate together. Once melting is done, spread the layer of chocolate evenly over already prepared two layers.
7. Put back the loaf pan in the refrigerator for half an hour. Once done take it out and cut it into slices. Serve the cold and sweet dessert.

VEGAN PECAN PIE

The specialty of this dish is that this pie contains chocolate and pecan. Making a vegan pie out of two is a bit tough but then there is one secret ingredient that can make this recipe simple. The secret one is tofu. If you have to make it more special, top it with a whipped cream.

Preparation Time: 1 hour
Serving Size: 8

INGREDIENTS:

- Vegan pie crust- 1
- Brown sugar- ½ cup
- Maple syrup- ½ cup
- Coconut oil- ¼ cup
- Vanilla extract- 1 tsp
- Tofu- ½ cup
- Coconut milk- ¼ cup
- Cocoa powder- ¼ cup
- Cornstarch- 2 tbsp
- Cinnamon- 1 tsp
- Salt- 1/4 tsp
- Pecan halves- 2 cups

DIRECTIONS:

1. Take a saucepan and mix maple syrup and brown sugar in it. Put this saucepan on medium flame and let it simmer for about 10 minutes. Keep stirring the content and make thick syrup out of it.
2. Take it off from heat and add some coconut oil and vanilla in the content.
3. Prepare the oven at 350 degree F.
4. Take a food processor bowl and put in cocoa powder, coconut milk, cornstarch, tofu, cinnamon and salt in it. Blend all the ingredients properly and make a smooth paste out of it.
5. Mix brown sugar and tofu mixture till everything blends completely. Put it in pecans.
6. Place all the mixture into pie crust and bake it for about 40 minutes.
7. Take it off from oven and let it cool completely. Serve delicious pie.

MINI VEGAN PIE

These are sweet and delicious surprises in small units. The crispy yet buttery crust of the pie will steal away your heart. The pie gets its sweetness from honey and the cherry of the pie is apple filling in the pie.

Preparation Time: 1 hour 40 minutes

Serving Size: 4

INGREDIENTS:

- Vegan pie dough- ½ recipe
- Apples- 2
- Honey- 1 tbsp.
- Brown sugar- 1 tbsp.
- Lemon juice- 1 tsp
- Cornstarch- ½ tsp
- Cinnamon- ½ tsp
- Sal- 1/2 tsp
- Butter- 1 tbsp.

Direction:

1. Make pie dough and keep it in freeze for about an hour.
2. Prepare oven at 400ºF. Take a mini pie dish and grease it with oil.
3. Take apple and peel it. Make 1/2cm cubes out of apple. Mix brown sugar, honey, cornstarch, lemon juice and cinnamon to appl. Mix everything evenly.
4. Cut 2/3rd of the pie so that it fits your pie dish exactly. If it hangs at the sides then you can trim the edges.
5. Put the apple mixture in the pie crust. Take remaining pie dough and make another circle of 1inch diameter at the top of dish. Put this one on the top of first one.
6. Seal the edges of the pie crust.
7. Place this in oven and bake it for 40 minutes. You will see a golden color on the top. Take it out of oven and let it rest for half hour. Enjoy.

CRANBERRY CAKE

This cake has a very moist texture and also has a slight bit of orange flavor. The top of the pie has a caramel flavor which balances the flavor of cranberry.

Preparation Time: 1 hour 15 minutes
Serving Size: 10

INGREDIENTS:

- Brown sugar- 3/4 cups
- Butter, divided- 3/4 cups
- Fresh cranberries- 12 Oz
- All-purpose flour- 1 3/4 cups
- Baking powder- 2 tsp
- Salt- 1/2 tsp
- Ginger, grounded- 1/2 tsp
- Cinnamon, grounded- 1/4 tsp
- Garlic cloves- 1/8 tsp
- Sugar- 1 1/2 cups
- Eggs- 3
- Orange zest- 1 tbsp
- Greek yogurt- 1/2 cup
- Milk- 1/4 cup
- Sugar for dusting
- Cranberries for garnish

DIRECTIONS:

1. Prepare oven till 350 degrees. Take a cake pan and grease the bottom of the pan.
2. Take a small saucepan and mix $1/4^{th}$ of butter and brown sugar. Keep this saucepan on flame and keep stirring the contents properly. Shift this mixture on the baking dish. On the top spread cranberries. Keep it aside.
3. Take another bowl and mix ginger, salt, cinnamon, baking powder, flour and cloves in it. Keep it aside.
4. In another bowl take ½ cup butter and sugar. Stir it continuously to make the content fluffy. Add egg into it and keep beating it. Mix orange zest in it.

5. Beat half of the dry ingredients and put Greek yogurt in it. Once beaten properly, put rest of the dry ingredient. Put milk in this. At the end batter should become smooth and consistent.
6. Put this batter in the cranberry cake, and spread it on the top. Put this in oven and bake it at 325 degree temperature. The cake should be baked for about 60 minutes. Once done keep it aside for about 10 minutes.
7. Take the cake out of the pan by keeping it from top side. Slice the cake into wedges. Sprinkle some powdered sugar and sugared cranberry from the top.

www.ingramcontent.com/pod-product-compliance
Lightning Source LLC
LaVergne TN
LVHW071927210226
832259LV00031B/207